DOWN THE
FOX HOLE

ALSO BY CHRIS WIDDOP

VELCRO THE NINJA KAT
Velcro: The Ninja Kat
Velcro: The Green Lion
Velcro: The Masquerade
Velcro: Polluted War
Velcro: The Egg Hunters

DOWN THE
FOX HOLE

CHRIS WIDDOP

Cover art by Christine Celenski
First Printing: 2025

ISBN 979-8-9876030-5-5

widdopc@velcrotheninjakat.com

www.VelcroTheNinjaKat.com

CONTENTS

BEYOND THE RISING SUN
1

ROAD TO MANIA
45

ANIME INSPIRED
53

THE SNOW QUEEN COMPILATION
59

THE TATTOO'S HEAT HAZE
65

A MEMORY OF SNOW
125

BEYOND THE RISING SUN

(The names of real people have been changed.)

Part I

Chapter I

In September of 2018, a friend from a wrestling forum that I still frequented shared one of Babymetal's music videos with me, and I decided to give it a watch. It was the video for their song *Gimme Chocolate*, and my first reaction was a bit mixed. I was initially put off by the cutesy opening to the song, but then as soon as the lead singer Su-metal began singing the chorus, I found myself suddenly intrigued. The music had a very anime-like sound to it, which I admired. And so, after the video ended, I started another one, this one for their song called *Karate*. The layout of the song was quite similar to that of *Gimme Chocolate*, so I was concerned if all of their songs were going to sound the same, like I had experienced with other bands in the past. But once I made it to my third video of theirs, *Megitsune*, I realized that initial assessment couldn't be further from the case.

I was thoroughly hooked at that point, and Babymetal would wind up being everything I never knew that I always wanted in a band.

Babymetal is a genre-blending Japanese J-pop/metal group consisting of three core members who sing and dance. Following this band is like following a live action anime series, with an ongoing story that plays out during their shows. Their shows unfold more like a stage production than a standard concert, with a revolving cast of characters based on the lore of the Fox God. I stayed up late binge watching videos of their live performances, before deciding to start from the beginning to catch up on all of their officially released live shows, similar to catching up on a long running anime.

Prior to discovering Babymetal, I was actually wondering when I might come across another band that would captivate me, since it's rare that a band connects with me in a way that I get excited enough to really dig deep into their musical library. In the past, other examples of musical artists that really clicked for me would include My Chemical Romance, Paramore, Muse, Avenged Sevenfold, and Sia. There's just something infectious and really refreshing about Babymetal. Watching their live performances is absolutely mesmerizing, with the three main band members frenetically moving around as they do their choreographed dance routines, all while maintaining a high level of energy and quality of singing night after night without ever missing a beat.

It wasn't long after getting into the band that I had determined I needed to see them live. I had never felt compelled to see other bands perform live, but with Babymetal, there was just something about their live show that I felt needed to be experienced in person. Shortly after I had finished catching up with the band's backlog of live events, they announced dates for their 2019 global tour. And the very first stop on their US leg of the tour was going to land in my home state in Orlando, Florida, and on my birthday at that.

Chapter II

I had just moved back home to Tallahassee, Florida, after a short stint living in New York. I was still getting myself situated, and one of the things that I needed was a job. So I reached out to a friend, Simon, who was working at a Publix grocery store just down the road from me, and we arranged to meet up at IHOP to catch up.

"Hey, it's been a while," I said.

"Yes sir!" beamed Simon, as he took his seat across from me. We discussed my time in New York for a bit, before the conversation moved on to how things had been going in town.

"So, do you think you could hook me up with a job at Publix?"

"I can see," said Simon. "I know some of the departments need help right now, so I'll talk to my manager and let you know."

"Thanks, I appreciate that," I said, before

changing the subject to more interesting topic matter. "So, have you heard of a band called Babymetal?"

I had him take out his phone and pull up their music video for the song *Megitsune*. Being a fellow anime fan, I had a feeling the band might be up his alley as well. He appeared to be impressed by what he heard, and he then did a quick search to pull up a video from his then current favorite anime My Hero Academia. It was a fan edited video cutting together scenes from the show, and playing a song from Babymetal over top of it, which we watched and enjoyed.

"You know, they'll be playing in Orlando this September," I told him. "Do you think you'd like to join me?"

"Hmm, that could be a possibility," said Simon. "I'll have to okay it with the wife first. I feel like she won't mind, though."

"Awesome," I said, "Well I'll let you know once tickets go on sale then."

"Sounds good."

* * *

Later that week I dressed up and I went to Publix to inquire about my job application. I met with the store's assistant manager, and he asked me if I was free for an interview right then. I told him that I was, and the next thing I knew I was brought into the manager's office for my job interview with both him and the store's produce manager. It went well, because they hired me on the spot, and I was definitely feeling a sense of relief, and a weight off my shoulders.

Once I made it back to my car I pulled out my phone to text the good news to Simon, but I was met by a missed text waiting for me from his wife. It read, "He's all yours. You two will make a cute couple. Good luck!" I was naturally very confused by this text.

She later explained in an e-mail that she was upset by how excited Simon was to be meeting with me when we reconnected the other night. I suppose they were going through some marital problems at the time, and this was the last straw for her, but I still felt unjustly attacked.

Initially I wrote a response where I tried to defend myself and how I felt she was putting me in an unfair position. But before I hit send I decided to leave the issue alone and I deleted my message.

Later that week tickets for the Babymetal tour went on sale. I didn't want to bother Simon at the time, and unnecessarily burden him during such a delicate situation with his wife. We hadn't spoken much since then, and I just asked him how things were and if we were still cool, and he assured me that we were. So I decided to go ahead and buy two tickets, and if things didn't work out then I'd just have to deal with it. There was another show taking place in Atlanta, Georgia, just two days later, so I went ahead and purchased a ticket for that show as well and I planned on flying solo.

A few days later I started my first day at the new job. It was also the first time I'd be seeing Simon in person since I got dragged into his marital problems, so I wasn't sure what to expect. Simon tried to play it off like nothing had happened, which was nice, but I still couldn't help but feel uncomfortable by the whole situation, which wasn't exactly the best way to start things off at a new job.

"I went ahead and bought your ticket," I told him.

"Okay," he said. "Well hopefully I'll be able to go, but I'll let you know."

"I gotcha," I said.

The months passed, and we were treating the situation like nothing had ever happened. I wasn't exactly okay with this, but I also didn't want to stir up the pot any more, so I decided to go along with it, as uncomfortable as it felt.

* * *

About a month prior to the show in Orlando, I met up with a fellow Babymetal fan named Samuel. We met through the internet, and decided to get together after we discovered we lived in the same city. We gathered at Moe's, and I ordered a burrito and sat across from him with anticipation of partaking in a satisfying conversation about Babymetal as we excitedly prepared for the upcoming show that we both planned to attend.

"I've been dying to meet someone else who's a fan," he said. "I just feel like I have so much to say!"

He wasn't lying about that. I barely got a word in during this conversation, as Samuel kept rattling on without taking a breath.

"After discovering Babymetal and following other Japanese groups like Sakura Gakuin, I decided to start learning Japanese," he said, before going into great detail about his journey learning a new language, including how he'd sometimes speak out loud in Japanese even while showering.

At some point he started talking about how

he worked at a small venue in town, and he told me several long winded stories about that job. And all the while, I mostly kept quiet and ate my burrito, only managing to get a word in here or there by interrupting his spiel during the rare opportune times to speak up.

We were seated in the restaurant for what felt like hours, and it seemed like we had barely even talked about Babymetal. Once it was starting to get late, though, I finally interrupted him one last time.

"Well, it's been fun, but I think I gotta get going," I said. "I've got an early shift at work tomorrow."

After we stepped outside our conversation continued on, and we discussed the prospects of meeting up again sometime.

"Maybe, we'll see," I said. "But I'll definitely see you at the show in Orlando!"

"For sure," he said, before extended his hand to me, which I responded to with a fist bump. We then parted ways, and I went home feeling completely drained from the encounter.

* * *

In the days leading up to the event hurricane

Dorian had formed, and the storm was predicted to directly hit Orlando the day before the show. There was of course concerns over what this meant for the fate of the performance, if it would be canceled or rescheduled, or if the show would go on. There were many people online voicing their concerns and calling for the band to back out, some even calling the band irresponsible for not calling off the show. But the band insisted that so long as the venue chose to remain open, they still intended to play. Thankfully the storm turned away and generally missed Orlando, so I was certainly grateful for that.

And then I received a text from Simon.

We had solidified our plans by this point, and were planning to attend the show together. In fact, he was even planning on driving us, since my car was acting up at the time and I didn't trust it to make a road trip from Tallahassee down to Orlando and then up to Atlanta and back home again. And while I wasn't entirely surprised by his text, I was still upset as I read his message that he was planning to drop out of the show, citing more personal issues at home. So now I was out both a friend to go to the show with, as well as my ride there.

On September 4th, 2019, the day of the show,

I scrambled and reached out to my mom, asking her if I could borrow her car for my trip. As a birthday present she allowed me to take her car down to Orlando, but she said that she would need it back after that, and so I'd have to drive my own car up to Atlanta. I was more than okay with that offer, and now with both the storm and my travel concerns behind me I was finally on the road to go see Babymetal in person.

Chapter III

I arrived in Orlando around mid-afternoon. When I was pulling up to Universal Orlando, where the venue was located, I saw that they had free parking after 6PM, so I decided to hang out in town until then. I found a local comic shop and browsed around a little, and while I was there I decided to reach out to Samuel to see if he had made it into town yet.

He had not.

Apparently he had canceled his hotel booking in response to the hurricane. I asked him if he was still going to try and make it down anyways, but he said that it was going to be too much of a hassle for him to do so at that point.

"It's okay," he assured me, "I'll just catch them the next time they come around."

I was dismayed by his response. After all, who was to say when next time would be?

* * *

When 6PM approached I made my way back to Universal to secure my parking spot, and I headed straight for the Hard Rock Cafe where the show would be taking place. I could see that there was already quite a long line of fans eagerly waiting to get inside. Before I took my place in line, I pulled out my phone and reached out to another local fan who I had recently connected with online. Her name was Kayla, and after learning I was making the trip to Orlando, she suggested that we could meet up. I texted her that I had arrived, and she told me where she was in line, and that I could find her wearing a blue shirt.

As I made my way to her, I decided to use some hand sanitizer.

"Hi, Kayla?" I asked, approaching the girl in the blue shirt.

"That's me."

"Nice to meet you," I said, then extended my hand out to her.

"Nice to meet-AHH!"

She instantly recoiled in disgust at the wet feel of the sanitizer that was still on my hand, and I felt like a fool.

"Oh, uh, sorry about that," I said.

We proceeded to have a very brief and awkward conversation after that, in which I learned that she'd be somewhere in the pit during the show. I suggested that we could perhaps meet back up after the show let out, and she said that we could maybe do that, though she didn't sound thrilled by the prospect.

I walked to the back of the line after that uncomfortable exchange. I tried to start up a conversation with the guy in front of me, but he didn't seem interested in talking, so I just kept to myself. I pulled out my phone and I informed my fellow fans via social media that I had arrived at the venue. Upon learning that it was also my birthday, the online fans took it upon themselves to dub the show "Legend – C", naming the show after me in honor of my special day.

Finally, the line started moving, and fans were filing into the venue. Since I had a seat for this particular show, I thankfully didn't have to worry about fighting for a good spot on the floor, so I took my time as I stepped inside. I visited the merch table and bought a Babymetal t-shirt and a towel, then I took my seat, where I was located front and center in the upper balcony.

My nerves were racked with excitement. Suddenly the lights dimmed, and the crowd erupted in thundering cheers, as the time had come for Babymetal to take the stage.

Chapter IV

Babymetal took to the stage with the song that initially proved to me that this band was the real deal, *Megitsune*. And man did they tear the house down right off the bat. Just seeing them stepping out on stage gave me chills, and experiencing their performance felt surreal. They followed this up with the live debut the of English version of *Elevator Girl*, a heavy hitting pop song about life's ups and downs, and then the Indian inspired *Shanti Shanti Shanti*, which were loads of fun, but then my mind was completely blown away by what followed.

This night saw the debut of the Gods of the West, or the western version of the Kami Band, who play the instrumentals in the band's live performances. As they started playing the next song, but before it really kicked in, a spotlight shined down on one of the guitarists, and he started playing a solo. And it actually took me a second for it to register what was happening, because I honestly couldn't believe it. Previously the Kami Band hadn't performed any solos in almost two years. So this alone was exciting enough, but after those solos ended the song kicked in proper with the return of the band's song *Kagerou*. Originally this song was a solo performance by the band's lead singer, Su-metal. But this time, after Su-metal took to the stage, she was then joined by Moametal and Riho on either side. As the three of them performed together with this new take of the song, my jaw dropped in amazement, and it remained that way the entire time.

This new reworked three person version of *Kagerou* was the highlight of the whole night for me. I seriously couldn't believe what I was seeing, from the Kami solos to the new choreography, this performance absolutely blew me away, and it definitely felt like a special moment being there in person on its debut night.

The emotionally driven *Starlight* came on next, which was then followed by *Future Metal*, which mostly acted as a nice little interlude to give the ladies a break, as the song was played over the speakers while a neat little video was shown to us, as opposed to being performed live. They then came back with their classic hit *Gimme Chocolate*, and this is when the crowd finally really came alive. Seeing this song live was definitely a blast, but the real party for me came next. When they started playing *Pa Pa Ya* I grabbed my newly purchased Babymetal towel and twirled it through the air like I was showing that hurricane how it's done. *Pa Pa Ya* was like a whirlwind to witness live, but the song was almost a blur after getting so intensely into it.

Distortion was next, and they introduced a new element that was actually pretty cool. On a number of songs, they had been utilizing a large LED screen behind them to provide backing graphics, such as the elevator effect during *Elevator Girl*, or the trippy patterns during *Shanti Shanti Shanti*. But for *Distortion*, they played the music video for the song behind the ladies during their performance, and it actually worked a lot better than one might expect. It just looked really cool seeing the band doing their choreography while this live action anime-like video played behind them, with cities being destroyed and the Chosen Seven being summoned and showing off their powers. And these cool backing effects continued with the song *Karate*, where they showed the ladies lighting on fire as they performed their martial arts inspired dance.

I mentioned how this show landed on my birthday, and the band had apparently caught wind of this, as up next we were treated to a much unexpected performance of the band's heavy metal birthday song, *Headbanger*. It had been years since this song had been performed outside of special occasions, so I was ridiculously excited to see it. One of their heavier songs, this one was absolutely sick to see performed live, and such a treat for my birthday.

Next up, we got this cool lore video showing us the formation of the Metal Galaxy, and this then lead directly into the song *The One*, a song about coming together as one. It started first with the unfinished version of the song performed by Su-metal, before the song really cranked up, and she was joined on stage by the other two. This one hit me pretty hard, and I was on the verge of tears throughout this entire performance.

The show closed out with an energetic performance of their power metal hit *Road of Resistance*, which left the crowd chanting for one more song as they cleared the stage. That was my first live Babymetal experience, and it completely exceeded my expectations. We got a number of surprises in the form of the updated *Kagerou* and

Headbanger, and the full set list was absolutely killer from top to bottom. By the end of it, my face was literally in pain from how hard I had been smiling for the past hour.

* * *

After the show had ended and the lights came up, people got up out of their seats and started making their way to the exits. I decided to linger a bit, and I turned around and sparked up an impromptu conversation with a couple who was seated behind me.

"Hey, I hope I didn't whack you with my towel during the show," I said.

"Nah, you're good," the guy assured me.

"That was awesome," I said. "I lost my mind with that Kagerou performance. And they even played Headbanger for my birthday!"

"Oh, it's your birthday," the guy's girlfriend asked.

"Yup!"

"Well happy birthday!"

"Thank you!"

"I'm just happy they played Gimme Choco-late," she said.

"Oh yeah, they were always going to play

that one," I said, suddenly aware that I was talking to more casual fans than myself. Still, it was a nice little interaction, and we said our farewells and parted ways.

After I exited the venue I pulled out my phone and I sent a text Kayla, to see if she was still around. She responded that she had already left. So with that, I made my lonely walk back to my car, and my even lonelier drive back home.

Part II

Chapter V

It was late when I arrived back home, and I crashed for the night. I slept in the next day, and I eventually got up and was back out onto the road to Atlanta. It was already dark by the time I arrived in town, and I drove by the venue to scope it out, and then I made my way to a nearby Walmart to sleep in my car for the night.

The next morning I woke up early in a desperate need to use the bathroom, and so I had to rush inside the Walmart to take care of business. My stomach was still giving me issues afterward though, so I bought some Pepto Bismol on the way out, and hoped that my bowels would behave and my body would hold up for the rest of the day.

I hopped over to a Target that was only about a mile away from the venue, and I decided to park my car there, and I hiked the rest of the way. Sometime around 9AM I had arrived at the Coca-

Cola Roxy, where that night's show was to take place, and there was already a small gathering of fans waiting around outside when I got there. Someone wrote a number on my hand to secure my place in line, and I began mingling with the crowd in our collective anticipation for the show.

I briefly spoke with a fan who was dressed as Pikachu. He had flown in from Germany, and was also at the show the previous night in Orlando. He told me he was planning on following the band for most of their tour dates.

I then met an older fellow dressed in tie-dye who I had recognized from the internet. His name was Marty, and he had also flown in for the show.

"You know, at one point, I knew people who used to worship the ground that Elvis Presley walked on," he mentioned. "At the time, I never understood it. But after discovering Babymetal? Yeah, I get it now."

I had to admit that I could get it to an extent, too.

Marty wandered off to talk to some other folks, and I got together with two younger fans named Felix and Turk. Felix was an Atlanta native, and had seen the band multiple times whenever they would play in town, and was wearing a shirt from their previous year's tour. Turk was in the military, and was currently on leave to see Baby-metal for the first time.

I spent most of the day hanging out under the shade of the trees with them, and we dove deep into a conversation about the band. In fact, Felix was surprised to learn that I had only gotten into the band recently.

"You know so much about them already, I would've figured you've been a fan for years," he said.

"Haha, nope, not yet."

Felix had mentioned how he had a crush on Moametal, and that she was his favorite member of the band.

"Are you planning on standing on her side of the stage?" I asked.

"Yeah, probably."

"How about you?" I asked Turk, who said that he'd likely try and find a spot on the same side of the stage as Felix.

"What about you?" Turk asked me back.

"Me?" I said. "I'm trying to get dead center, as close to the stage as I can."

* * *

The sunny day wore on, and before we

knew it, a massive line of fans had formed. And there I was, right near the front of that line.

I met some other fans that I had initially met online, including Bam, who like me also drove in from out of state, and who told me that he'd see me in the pit before taking his spot in line.

Meanwhile, Marty had made his way back up to where we were standing, and he mentioned how he had spoken to a few people who were only there to see the opening band, but who were planning on leaving before Babymetal hit the stage. "I told them to stick around, though. Just give 'em a chance." He nodded his head, hopeful that the fans would heed his advice.

Marty then pulled out a shirt with a picture of a tomato on it. "I brought this in memory of a friend who passed recently," he said. "I was going to hang this over the railing, so that a piece of him could attend the show along with us, since he can't be here." He asked me if I'd take a picture of it for him once we were inside, and I agreed to do so.

I turned back to Felix and Turk, and Turk was looking especially anxious waiting in line.

"I don't know how to explain it, but it's like I feel nervous," Turk said. "Does that make sense?"

"Yeah, I get that. I feel it, too," I said.

We then heard someone ahead of us in line

who was explaining how he used to be a security guard, and how he once accidentally met Babymetal backstage, back before he was even a fan. He mentioned how Yuimetal was still in the band at the time, and this got us all discussing who everybody thought that night's Avenger would be.

To explain, about a year prior, one of the original members of the band, Yuimetal, had officially made her departure from the group. After the fact, in order to fill her empty spot on stage, the band had incorporated a system of rotating backup dancers, where each night a different dancer would fill in the spot, and you were never entirely sure who it would be on a given night. These backup dancers were referred to as Avengers, and in Orlando, Riho had filled in the role as that's night Avenger. But for this night, we weren't sure if it would be her again, or one of the other two Avengers, Momoko or Kano.

"Momoko? Fifty/fifty," said the former security guard. "Kano? Zero chance."

We all agreed with his assessment, since Kano was the youngest and least likely the venture outside of Japan, but it still wasn't certain if Momoko had traveled with them on this tour.

Shortly after this discussion the doors finally opened up, and they started letting fans inside.

First they let in the VIP ticket holders, and I was right in the front of the line for the fans entering next. We were all really nervous, but we were ready. And finally they called us up, and we made our way inside the venue.

* * *

I was shocked by just how good a spot I wound up landing. I was in the second row behind the barrier, dead center, and directly behind the former security guard who we were talking to outside. A fellow fan wearing a fox mask then stepped up beside me, and I turned to see as Felix and Turk grabbed their spots off to the right side of the stage.

It wasn't long before the place was completely packed. As I turned to look behind me, I could see Pikachu was standing right in the center of the pit, and I also caught Bam somewhere, who smiled and waved back at me. As I looked up to the stands, I could see Marty take his seat in the front row off to the right. He draped the tomato shirt over the railing, and as promised, I took a picture of it for him.

I turned to face the stage. Then the lights went out, and the crowd erupted in cheers.

Chapter VI

It wasn't long after Babymetal took to the stage when I discovered first hand about the intense crush of people in the pit area. As soon as those three ladies stepped out, the crowd suddenly stampeded towards the stage, and everyone was pushing forward all at once. It was crazy, with people literally climbing over each other, and soon I realized that I had somehow been pushed back a couple rows, never really noticing it was even happening until it had already happened. Needless to say, I had lost track of my friends amidst all of the chaos.

But seeing the ladies so close was just unreal, and I seriously couldn't believe they were really right there, so close before my eyes. It turned out that Riho was the Avenger again on this night. And they all projected a striking, larger than life presence, which totally commanded my attention as they filed out onto the stage for *Megitsune*. Being this close to the stage, I could really see all of the details that I missed sitting in the stands in Orlando. Details such as Moametal making a silly face at Su-metal during *Megitstune*, or all the other funny faces she made during *Shanti Shanti Shanti*, or how the black strands on the back of the bassist's mask would blow in the air behind him, or Su-metal's wild smiles during her dance in the rap portion of *Pa Pa Ya*.

Being in that pit was like nothing I've ever experienced at a concert. I mean, I have been in my fair share of mosh pits before, but the energy in this crowd was on a whole different level. The sheer intensity was nonstop, and the crowd was totally into it, jumping around and pumping their fists in the air, all while singing and screaming along with the songs, and keeping up with the intensity of the dancing on stage. And I was right there with them the whole time.

When I initially purchased my tickets for the tour, I purposefully chose to get a seat for the first show, and a pit ticket for the other, just to ensure that I would get a different experience from them. And man was it ever. The energy in this crowd was off the charts, and being down in that pit felt like we were truly as much a part of the show as the band was on the stage.

Before going to this show there was a part of me that found it curious why people would want to attend a Babymetal concert just to wind up in one of the circle pits, or somewhere in the venue where you can't even really see the show, despite how much of it is so visually based around the dancing and the lighting and video effects. But after experiencing this show first hand, I understand now that being there live is a totally different experience than watching one of their shows in the comfort of your own home.

When I am watching a show at home I can really digest the music and the choreography, and take everything in as it unfolds. But being there live, you really do just get so immersed in a whirlwind as the music and the crowd become one. It's suddenly not so much about watching the show, but rather, being a part of the show, and singing along and pulling your own weight, following Su-metal's commands to jump and scream and dance. I mentioned how *Pa Pa Ya* in Orlando was like a blur after I had gotten so into it, and honestly, that sorta describes this whole show from the pit. Being in that crowd felt like being in the middle of a raging storm, with your adrenaline pumping so wildly that you barely have a moment to properly register everything that's happening all around you.

They say that Babymetal doesn't come out to perform, but rather they come out to battle. And that's what each of their shows is like, with a new battle being waged in their ongoing Metal Resistance. Having been in that crowd, that definitely feels like an apt description, because it certainly feels like a battle is taking place in that pit, though it's one where we're all fighting toward a common goal. Although we are all drenched in sweat and ready to collapse from the integrel part we've all played in the show, before you know it an hour has already passed, yet it feels like it has all happened in a flash.

Just like watching their shows is unlike watching any other band I've ever seen, being there live is very much the same. There's just something intensely euphoric about it, something that just transports you to another plane. It's honestly hard to even explain what a heavy hitting and all around out of this world experience a Babymetal concert is, you really have to just go to one of their shows to see for yourself.

Because the show was such a workout, songs such as *Future Metal* were a nice break for the band and the audience as well, just to give us all a chance to catch our breath a little. But still, there's nothing quite like being in that crowd as we were all bowing down to Su-metal during *Headbanger*, or relentlessly twirling our towels through the air during *Pa Pa Ya*, or pumping our fists in the air in unison as we sing along to *Road of Resistance*.

The one song I didn't really participate in too much at this show though was *The One*. But that's because I wanted to step back and take in that moment to really appreciate their performance, and be swept away by the emotion of the song. During this song there was a brief moment when Su-metal's eyes were scanning the crowd, and she happened to look down at me just as I was staring up at her with awe. Su-metal looked wonderfully majestic up there on her own.

So despite playing the exact same set as the previous show in Orlando, my experience with this show in Atlanta was completely different. The crowd showed an intensity that was honestly missing in Orlando, and being in that pit was almost like entering a whole other world. And really being a part of the show on this level gave me a whole new perspective, particularly once we reach the finish line and Su-metal screams "We are!" and we all scream back, "Babymetal!" Because in that moment, that statement brings on a whole

new meaning, like we've really earned our place in
The One.

Chapter VII

After the show let out and the fans began to scatter, I was able to catch sight of Felix and Turk. I caught back up with them and shared in the excitement of the battle that had brought us all together.

I then made my way outside, where I overheard Bam talking with someone else about how emotional an experience it was to see *Starlight* performed live. I joined up with his group and once more revelled in celebration along with them, when Marty stepped up and said that Babymetal has never been better.

Originally, there were plans for an afterparty to be held at a bar and grill across the street from the venue, but there was an Atlanta Braves game that night, and the place was already packed to capacity with Braves fans by the time our show let out. I still went up to the bar and downed several cups of water to rehydrate myself though, and then a group of us got back together as we made our way down the street.

One by one, each of my new friends headed for their destinations, and soon it was my turn to part ways. So I said my farewells and walked back to my car.

I attempted to drive back home that same night, but I was so worn out that I had to pull over about halfway there. I caught a few hours of sleep in another Walmart parking lot, then woke up feeling like I had partaken in a full body workout the night prior. I jested online that I'd have to get in better shape for the next show, then I was back on the road once more.

The whole way home I relived the experience in my head, and I was glad that I was able to go on such an amazing adventure, and ready to do it all over again.

ROAD TO MANIA

From the late '90s until about the mid 2000s, I was absolutely obsessed with wrestling. It all started when my family rented a copy of WCW vs. nWo: World Tour for the N64 one weekend. We enjoyed the game so much that we decided to watch some actual wrestling matches. We initially started watching WCW, but within just a week or so, we had already changed over to WWF, now WWE. I quickly became a diehard fan, and I would watch it religiously for the next decade or so. Beyond the physicality of the in ring action, I was really drawn to the characters and the storytelling, both inside the ring and out, and really just the whole theatrics of it all. To this day I still keep up with it, even though I'm not a hardcore fan anymore. I followed it passionately, watching as much of it as I could possibly see. I particularly liked keeping up with all the big promotions during that period.

That all changed when I joined the Marines

in the summer of 2005.

A friend from high school and fellow wrestling enthusiast, Derrick, had plans to enlist in the Marine Corps, and he succeeded in pressuring me to join as well. Obviously, during training periods I wasn't able to watch any wrestling, so I had to just do without. And unfortunately, that included missing WrestleMania season.

I was especially bummed out that I was going to miss the biggest wrestling show of the year as it was airing live, and I decided that the only way to make up for it was to attend WrestleMania in person the following year. So I called up Derrick, and we made plans to do precisely that.

* * *

We purchased our tickets for the show as soon as they went on sale. By this time I was back living at home in Tallahassee, Florida, so we were going to have close to a 1,000 mile long trip to get to the venue. A year later, in the spring of 2007, we were on our way to see WrestleMania 23 live in Detroit, Michigan.

Initially, Derrick and I booked a bus to get up to Detroit. All went well on the first half of the trip. But then we had to change buses for the remainder of the ride. It was the middle of the night when we got dropped off at the bus station, and the place was extremely packed. We weren't sure where to go to transfer to the next bus, and the line for customer service was several hours long. It was so loud that it was impossible to make out any of the announcements or find where we needed to be, and after a while, it was clear that we had missed our bus.

So at this point we called for a taxi, and we went to the airport. We booked our tickets for the remainder of the way, and we were finally back on track. Though our seats on the flight were separated, Derrick tried to sit next to me anyways. However, this didn't work out when the person whose seat he had taken showed up shortly afterwards, so we were separated the remainder of the flight. I just took a nap, and before I knew it, we were landing safely in Detroit.

Our next stop was the hotel, and that's when we ran into our next hiccup. Apparently, we had accidentally booked a hotel that was just over the border in Canada. So we had to re-book another hotel that was actually in Detroit, and we managed to find a place not too far from the Ford Field, where WrestleMania 23 would be taking place the following day.

That next day it was bright and sunny, without a cloud in the sky. We decided to walk from our hotel to the stadium, and once we arrived we had fun mingling with other fans outside in eager anticipation of the show, and catching glimpses of various wrestlers arriving at the venue.

When they opened the gates we filed inside and made our way to our seats. We had an awesome night watching the spectacle of WrestleMania transpire before our amazed eyes.

* * *

After the show, we made the risky decision to walk back to our hotel in the middle of the night in the streets of Detroit. Thankfully we made it back without issue. Then the following day, it was back to the bus station for the long trip back home. We grabbed our seats at the back of the bus, where I spent the majority of the trip sleeping, and we made it back home without any of the trouble we had experienced on the way up.

Ironically, right before the show they announced that WrestleMania XXIV would be taking place in Orlando, Florida, which is just a short drive away where I lived. Had we known at the time that we purchased our tickets that WrestleMania was going to be in our home state the following year, we likely would've just waited for that show. Nevertheless, we didn't regret venturing so far to go see WrestleMania. It was definitely worth all the trouble, and we made memories along the way that would last a lifetime.

ANIME INSPIRED

It's one thing to travel out of town to see a concert or a wrestling show, but how about a movie? Well that is just what I did back in the winter of 2015 when I drove three hours out of town from Tallahassee to Ocala, Florida, to the nearest screening of the latest Naruto movie, titled *Boruto: Naruto the Movie*.

This was still in the early days of anime movies being released internationally close to the same time as they were initially released in Japan. Thankfully nowadays we regularly get anime movies released theatrically in the U.S., but back then it was uncommon. Oftentimes fans would have to wait at least a year or so to see new anime movies released domestically, and even then it was very rare that they would be released widely in theaters. But this was one of the few Naruto movies to release theatrically Stateside, and the first one to play at a theater that was anywhere close to me. So I of course jumped at the opportunity to take the trip down to see it only a month after its Japanese release, otherwise I would have to wait another year to see it on DVD.

The movie itself was the best of all of the Naruto movies, probably the closest we'll get to a perfect Naruto movie, and it was well worth the trip. In fact, structurally the film felt like a perfect template to follow should anyone try to adapt the series into live action, which was a personal dream of mine at one point.

Not long after I had first gotten into Naruto, I was forming ideas on how the series might translate into a live action film adaptation. I got as far as forming a plan to make a short film based on the series, but over time I chose instead to use some of the ideas I had and incorporate them into an original project. I came up with a story that was based in reality, but that also incorporated a little bit of fantasy.

For the fantasy aspects of the movie I planned to film several dream sequences, and I imagined each of them would be like a mini music video. The idea for this came from my love of anime openings, and how they tell a story through visuals and music alone, setting the tone for the show you're about to watch. I wanted to take that aspect and utilize it to help tell my own story. The initial script incorporated a number of elements that I had no realistic way of filming at the time, such as scenes involving characters flying around and walking on water. I eventually whittled down the first draft into something more reasonable to accomplish.

In addition to Naruto, I also borrowed elements from some other anime shows I was into at the time, such as Bleach and FLCL, and the end result was my first short film, titled *The Red Scarf*, which was released in the summer of 2012.

I'm still proud of this movie today, and even though I've arguably gone on to make technically better film projects, it's still my favorite. It has always been rewarding to see other people pick up on the various aspects of the film inspired by anime, just like one might recognize classic film references while watching a Quentin Tarantino flick.

While the dream of making a live action Naruto movie has faded, I definitely still value the creative inspiration that the series has brought to me over the years. And making the long trip to watch that Naruto movie on the big screen for the first time was a great reminder of that creative catalyst.

THE SNOW QUEEN COMPILATION

In the summer of 2014, I went to Alabama, where I was planning on attending an anime convention to sell my Velcro the Ninja Kat books at a table I had reserved. The show was called Hamacon, and it was taking place in downtown Huntsville. I regularly sold my books at various conventions back then, and at one of them I had met a lovely lady named Nikki. We kept in touch over the years, and since she also lived in Alabama, I planned on bringing her to this event to help run my table with me. So I picked Nikki up on my way there, and we were off to Hamacon.

During the drive there we began discussing the movie *Frozen*, which had come out about a half year prior. We were talking about the various fan theories that had sprung up since the movie's release. As we talked I started gushing about every aspect of the movie, and how relatable I found the story and the characters, particularly the Snow Queen.

It was sometime during this conversation that it dawned on me that *Frozen* had become my all time favorite movie. And it was a satisfying realization, as I never really had a definitive answer to that age old question, "What's your favorite movie?" I had a number of movies that I might say were my favorite, such as *Independence Day*, *The Dark Knight*, and *Revenge of the Sith*, but no one specific film that I could cite with confidence. Until *Frozen*.

I am not saying that I think *Frozen* is the "best" movie I've ever seen, since I could certainly point out a number of technical flaws. Nevertheless, I actually find its imperfections charming. The essence of this movie is found in its characters. The magical ways in which it explores these characters' depths is unlike anything I've ever seen.

* * *

We arrived at the convention and set up our table. As we looked around at all the participants throughout the day, our conversation turned to what were our favorite cosplays we had seen so far. I mentioned someone who was dressed up as a perfect Snow Queen. I had noticed that, much to my surprise, Snow Queens had been relatively uncommon at all of the conventions I had attended recently. But every time one did appear, it was as if time suddenly stood still, and all eyes would be drawn to her stunning presence.

Nikki smiled at my recollection, and an idea had sprung to mind. We decided that I should try to take a picture with every Snow Queen cosplayer that we happened to come across, and compile the collection online, like a running gag or a meme. Nikki loved the idea, and urged me to follow through with the plan. We initially dubbed this exercise The Snow Queen Project, and it was off to the races scanning the crowd of attendees for any Snow Queen cosplayers we could find.

At this first show we managed to find a handful of traditionally dressed Snow Queens who agreed to pose with me for a photo. As we moved forward with the project at other conventions we found a wide variety of Snow Queens who were also happy to pose.

The Snow Queens we saw were donned in all the character's various dresses from the film, and they came in every shape and size that you could imagine. We found skinny Snow Queens, and plump Snow Queens; tall Snow Queens, and short Snow Queens; young Snow Queens, and old Snow Queens; a hipster Snow Queen, and a heavy metal Snow Queen; a rainbow Snow Queen, and a fire Snow Queen; a sci-fi Snow Queen, and a Deadpool Snow Queen. We even found a couple of male Snow Queens.

After finishing our project of The Snow Queen Compilation, it was gratifying to see first hand just how many other people were similarly affected by my favorite character in the movie. It was amazing that so many people found something about the Snow Queen that they could relate to, that inspired them to put their own spin on the character. And after we organized this photo project and posted it online, people responded with the same joy we had experienced when we were making the photos.

Still though, how cool would it be to somehow someday meet the real Snow Queen?

THE TATTOO'S
HEAT HAZE

2006
The W Tattoo

It's sort of funny, with the exception of one of my tattoos that I'll discuss later, most of my work is fairly concealed under my clothes, so a lot the time people don't even realize just how many tattoos I have. For me personally, I don't get my tattoos to make a fashion statement, I get them for myself. And yet despite keeping them quite private, here I am about to finally share and discuss my tattoos in depth.

It was early 2006, and I was home in Tallahassee and ready to get my first tattoo. I had wanted tattoos since I was a kid, and when it came to my first tattoo, I thought it would be a good idea to start off with something simple.

My older brother, Adam, already had a number of tattoos by this point, and one of the tattoos he had was an old English W on his right inner bicep, which stood for our last name. So I figured I could get this same tattoo in the same spot. The idea was that eventually perhaps the rest of our brothers would get this same tattoo as well, and it could be something that sort of connected us, a family tattoo that we all shared. Unfortunately, that did not wind up coming to pass.

Adam went with me to Euphoria Tattoos, the shop where I would wind up getting most of my work done. I met with my artist, Alain, who would also go on to do most of the work on my body. It was a quick enough session that took only half an hour. It didn't really hurt, and I recall it feeling more irritating than actually painful. But I got my work done, and it was just the beginning of my tattoo journey to come.

I don't recall to this day every tattoo idea I ever had when I was younger, but there are at least a couple of them that I have a permanent reminder of, as they wound up being tattoos that I would get later in life. I'm a pretty firm believer in wanting my tattoos to hold meaning to me, and I feel like my pieces act as expressions of especial passions and personal anecdotes in my life's story. Over the years, I would develop personal rules for what justifies getting a piece tattooed, and I would face the regretful consequences that would come with breaking those rules.

2007
The Madness Tattoo

My high school nickname given to me by my peers was Madman Chris. Depending on who you ask, other people might say that my nickname was something other than that, but this was the one that stuck, and the one I embraced the most, as I felt it was a pretty cool name to have. I suppose I was a bit of a weird kid, even among other weird kids. But I still managed to make some friends regardless, and they often championed my odd behavior and sometimes controversial sense of humor and way of thinking.

For me personally, I would continue to adopt the name Madman, though it evolved into Madness. The first step of this evolution came about as a result of create-a-wrestler modes in WWF video games such as Wrestlemania 2000 and

No Mercy, where I named my self-insert created wrestler Chris Madness. Had I ever followed through on my former aspirations to become a professional wrestler myself, that's likely the name I would've gone on to wrestle under.

Eventually I dropped the first name, and Madness has been a name that I've used to describe a number of my creative endeavors, most notably (and perhaps most fittingly) naming my internet blog This is Madness, where I would often share my unique and sometimes controversial thoughts, which originally started in 2005.

A little over a year had passed since I had gotten my first tattoo, and I was getting the itch for another one. I had a few ideas, some that were more complicated than others, but as would become a trend for a number of my earlier tattoos, I decided to continue and keep things simple for the time being. And so, for my next tattoo, I decided upon getting that old school nickname, or at least its post-school evolution, permanently etched onto my skin.

I decided to get the word spelled vertically down my ribs on the left side of my body, which felt like an appropriately unconventional place-ment and stylization. Like the W, it was a pretty quick process, and surprisingly to me, also relatively painless. I went to a different artist for this one, but one still at Euphoria, and I was very pleased with the end result.

It was also around this time that I came up with my "one year" rule, where in order to allow myself to get a tattoo, it needed to be an idea that I still wanted at least a year later, and I was only going to allow myself to get one tattoo per year. This way, my art could tell the story of my life as the years passed on, as opposed to my body being a canvas dedicated to merely a single period in my life.

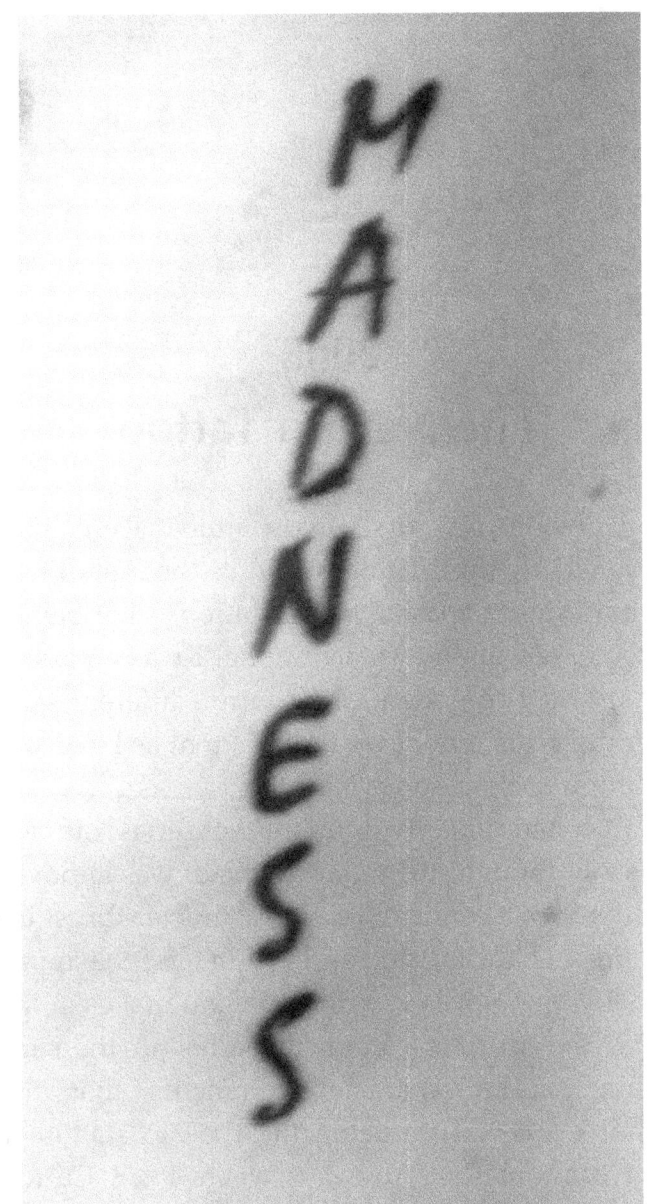

73

2008
The Naruto Tattoo

While my first two tattoos were more personal, my third tattoo would be the first of what I would describe as a "fanatic tattoo", that being a tattoo based upon a franchise that I was a passionate fan of. I've gotten into a lot of different series over the years, but never to the extent as I had with the popular ninja series Naruto.

I had initially written the series off, as I foolishly thought the main character was annoying and felt like a comic relief side character thrust into the main character slot, and I didn't see the appeal. Funnily enough, even the manga makes a gag about this during a moment earlier in the series where another character comments that they couldn't see Naruto being the type to star in his own comic series. Anyways, years later, Cartoon

Network was running a marathon of the Naruto anime, which they called the Naruto Hundo, and after catching a couple of episodes I was instantly hooked, and had a complete 180 on the series. I then went back and both watched and read all the earlier episodes of the anime and the manga, and I continued to keep up with it until the series' conclusion.

This was the first time I was so hooked that I went out of my way to download foreign episodes, and certainly the first time I ever picked up the original manga after getting into an anime. It wasn't long before I was all caught up on the series and fully invested, and with that investment came my desire to invest in a tattoo commemorating my passion.

Still not quite ready to commit to anything too complex yet, I decided to go with a simpler design from the series. There are a number of different symbols and marks that some of the characters featured on their bodies, but I gravitated most to the Anbu insignia. It's a spiral shaped symbol, and a relatively simple tattoo that characters in the series who are a member of the Anbu special military unit wear on their left shoulder.

After a year had passed and I still wanted the tattoo, I went back up to the shop and got the work done. The same artist who did my Madness tattoo also did this one, and it was another quick, easy, and relatively pain-free experience.

2009
The Great Mosquito Tattoo

The Great Mosquito is an original character that I made up. Its initial origins though, not unlike Chris Madness, lie with WWF video games. I pretty much created a mirror character of Chris Jericho, and just added a gas mask of some sort on him, and named this character The Great Mosquito. I would continue to use this name for wrestling characters in various online e-feds I would participate in during my high school years, and would later make the character a more literal mosquito as I incorporated it into other fictional works. A running gag I had in regard to The Great Mosquito being a Mexican Mariachi in addition to a wrestler also lead to my occasionally referring to him as El Squito, which is where the name El came about when I would wind up working the character into my Velcro the Ninja Kat series as a primary antagonist.

Some of my friends in high school were aware of this character of mine, and one of them wound up becoming a tattoo artist at Euphoria. His name was Kane, and the moment I went in and told him I wanted to get a tattoo of The Great Mosquito, he already knew exactly what I had in mind.

This was a tattoo where most of my time putting together the idea concerned its placement on my body. It was going to be yet another smaller and simpler one, but I wasn't entirely sure where it would look best. I wound up deciding upon my left wrist, which in turn would make it my most visible tattoo, so we had to get it right.

Thankfully, Kane was up to the task, and when I went in for my appointment, he showed me his sketch, and I loved it. It was a mosquito drawn in a bit of a more traditional tattoo style, and showing him sucking the blood out of my wrist. The original tattoo had a bit of color subtly shaded into it, though over the years that would all fade away. The image itself still remains though, and it's one that I've been more than satisfied with.

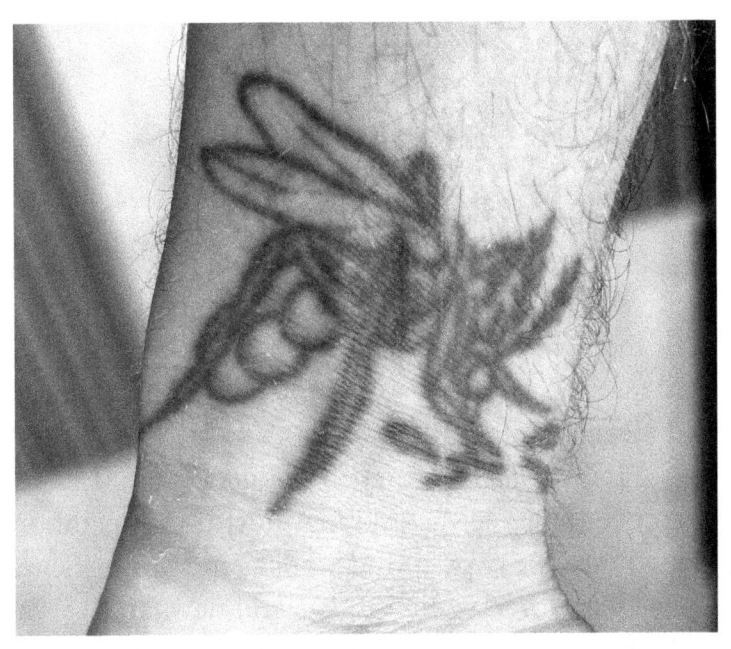

2010
The Sonic the Hedgehog Tattoo

Up to this point, I had continued to stick with the simpler designs for my tattoos, but now I was ready to move up to something a bit bigger and more ambitious.

I am a *huge* Sonic the Hedgehog fan. I have been ever since I was a kid. A next door neighbor loaned us their copy of the Sonic game for the Sega Genesis way back when it was still new, and I was instantly hooked. Years later, another neighborhood friend introduced me to the Archie comic series, which only further cemented my love for the franchise. I loved the games, I loved the cartoons, and I was an especially big fan of the Archie comic book run. One of my favorite stories in the Archie comic was titled Mecha Madness, a story which saw the blue hedgehog get roboticized, thus becoming Mecha Sonic in the process, and forced to battle against his friends against his will.

The story was well told, and the art was fantastic, particularly the cover art depicting this story. In fact, I actually realized that, when wrapped around in the shape of my lower leg, the design on the cover for the Mecha Madness special (which was essentially a collage of most of the primary Sonic cast) left just enough room to fit in the design of Mecha Sonic from the initial cover of the story from issue #39. So I knew that was what I wanted, wrapped around my left leg, was this combined collage of characters from the series. I also figured that Mecha Madness tied in well with the theme started with my earlier Madness tattoo, so it was definitely the way to go.

I always knew that if I were to get a Sonic tattoo, I would want to get it on my leg, because Sonic is known for his fast running, so where better to get a tattoo of the speedster? I came up with the idea for this particular tattoo several years back, so it had *long* surpassed my "one year" test. I had been waiting to get this tattoo since before I ever even got my W.

I went back to Alain for this one, my original

artist who did that first tattoo, and I showed him my idea. He was skeptical at first, since there was a lot of small details he wasn't confident would come out right. But after scheduling an appointment with him, by the time I showed up for our first session, he had since grown a whole new confidence, and was certain he could pull it off, which definitely set me at ease.

He initially quoted it as being a ten hour project, but he managed to complete the work in closer to six hours over the course of three or four sessions. I would also say that this was my first truly *painful* tattoo, as once he started work on the meatier area on the back side of my leg, I was in agony. But I was thrilled with the end result. This would go on to become by far my most popular tattoo, one that often received a wowed response when people would see it, and one that family and friends would even brag about to other people.

Being my first fully colored tattoo, I also learned over time that different colors of ink respond differently from person to person. And for me, I learned that red takes longer to heal than other colors do, and I also learned that brown fades out much quicker on me than other colors. This would become even more evident with another tattoo I would wind up getting later on down the line.

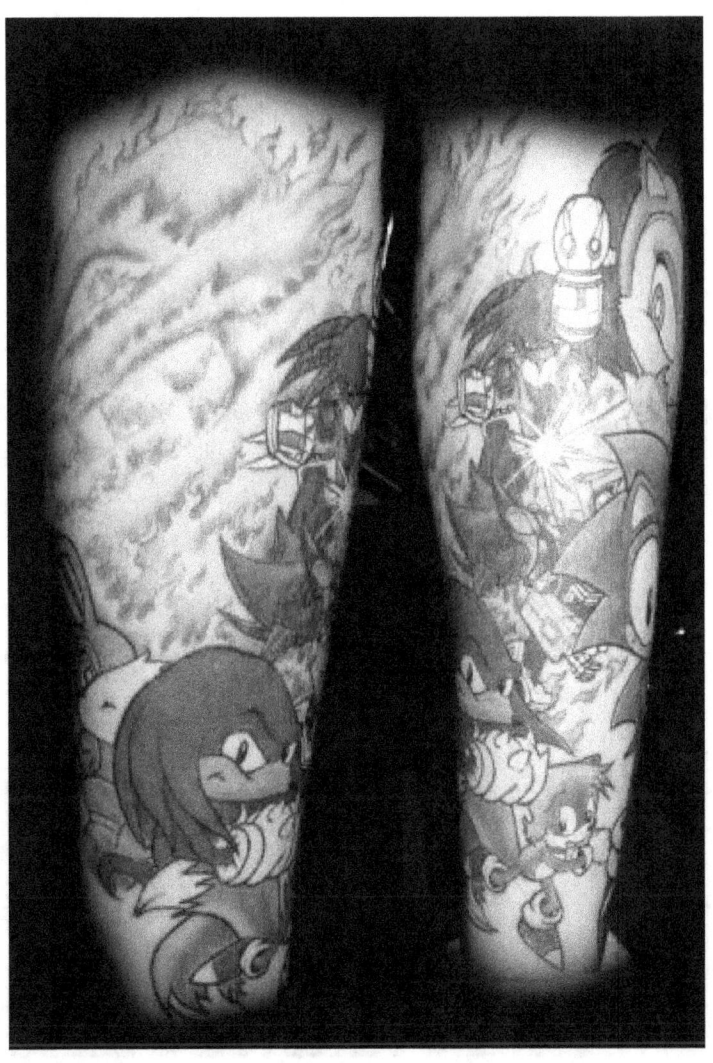

84

2010
The Abraham Lincoln, Wrestling Champion Tattoo

Rules exist for a reason, and I learned that first hand after breaking my own. In addition to breaking the rule of only one tattoo per year, I also broke the rule requiring I still want a specific tattoo a year after coming up with the idea for it before committing to it. And I wound up paying the price for these mistakes.

It was November of 2010. Earlier in the year, I had already gotten my Sonic tattoo, and I was already feeling the itch for something new. I was knee deep in my third National Novel Writing Month (or NaNoWriMo), and I decided I was going to be a bit more spontaneous than usual, and get something to represent my creative aspirations to commemorate the occasion.

Back when I was in high school, I had written a screenplay for a short film featuring Abraham Lincoln taking on John Wilkes Booth in a wrestling match. This was in part inspired by my absolute obsession with wrestling at the time, as well as the knowledge that Abraham Lincoln was apparently a professional wrestler himself back in his day. That short film sadly never came to pass, but I still liked the idea, and thought it would be a neat idea for a tattoo. I also figured that it could be a cool way to get a tattoo showcasing my passion for wrestling, since the idea of getting a tattoo dedicated to a specific wrestler or wrestling organization always felt a bit off for me.

I decided to give a different artist at a different shop a chance for this new idea, someone who came highly recommended to me. I was met with a lot of red flags by the artist early on, but I disregarded them, and decided to push through anyways. I presented the artist with my idea, which was to see Abe Lincoln standing victorious, holding up a wrestling championship into the air after having defeated John Wilkes Booth in the ring, which I wanted to get just above my right knee.

The tattoo was finished in two sessions. The

first session he focused on just Lincoln himself, and it looked decent enough so far. Session two saw him adding in the rest of the details, and I started getting worried as he continued working. The piece was much darker than I was expecting, and I made my concerns known once he started coloring in the wrestling mat black. He assured me it would look right once it healed, but that wouldn't be the case.

In terms of pain, this one was up there as well, not too dissimilar from the back of my left leg. And the end result of the actual work was kind of a mess, and mostly just looked like a big black spot on my upper leg. I suppose the silver lining was that it was at least in a very easily hidden spot, as I'm not exactly known for wearing shorts, but this was the first time I was very displeased with my tattoo.

I would go on to spend the next decade ruminating how I could go about fixing it, whether to get a cover-up, which would require something at least equally large and dark, or through expensive laser removal. I suppose it could be worse. After all, my oldest step-brother, John, got his girlfriend's name tattooed across his chest in bold, and he had to get a whole chest piece to cover it after they broke up. But even so, I learned a lot from this experience. I learned not to break my own rules again, and I also learned not to ignore red flags and rush into things if I'm not gelling well with an artist, even if they do come highly recommended.

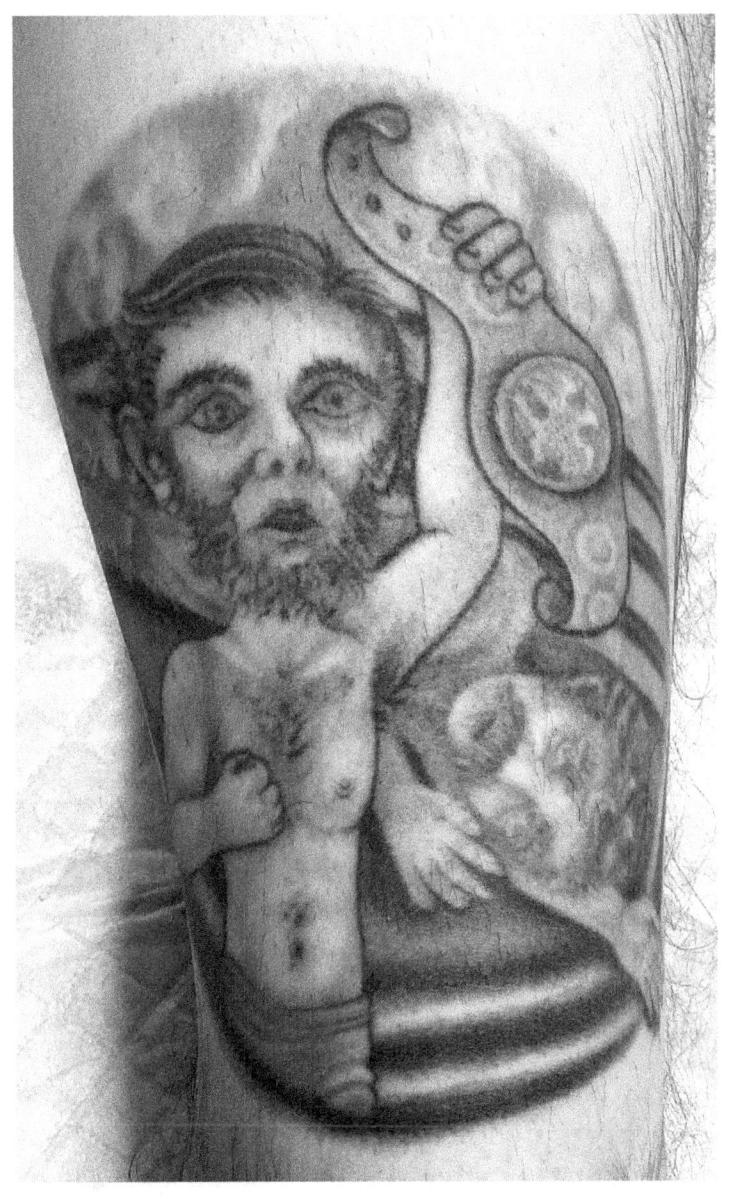

2011
The Velcro Tattoo

On August 6th, 2011, my cat Velcro passed away. I'd had her since I was a child, and she was a huge part of my life growing up. Shortly after she passed, I decided to get a tattoo in her memory. In truth, I had been planning to get a tattoo dedicated to my cat for a number of years by this point, but I hadn't gotten around to it before then.

It was a picture of her face, tattooed on my chest, just over my heart. I had to dig out some old photos of her to bring to the artist. I didn't have a smart phone yet at the time, otherwise I'd certainly have a lot more pictures of her than I do. But I brought a couple up to the shop, where I once again went to Alain (who would do the remainder of my work from here on out), and we picked out the shot that would make for the best quality piece.

This is certainly my most personal tattoo to date. Not a lot of people have seen it, but it's one that I see every day when I'm standing in front of the mirror. And it's nice being able to glance down and see my cat's face every day, even long after she's gone.

I was glad to have been able to spend the previous three years living alone in my trailer with her, as she always wanted to be an only cat. But even though I wound up having to move back home shortly before she passed, I was still thankful to be there all the same, since I was in a place where I could feel safe and comfortable, and having just left my previous job not long prior, I had the privilege of not having to work through my grief.

A year later I would finally release the first book in my Velcro the Ninja Kat series, a story I had been working on since I was a child, and I would finally be able to share my love for my cat with the world. She was a brown cat, and as I mentioned before, brown ink tends to fade away faster than other colors on my skin, so a lot of the color has already faded out. But even so, for me personally, even as she continues to fade, I'll always hold a piece of her with me in my heart.

2016
The Frozen Tattoo

We jump ahead a number of years before I got my next tattoo. I guess a lot of my ideas in the meantime kept failing my "one year" rule, and so I kept holding off. That was until in the winter of 2013 I watched a movie called *Frozen*, based on the fairy tale The Snow Queen by Hans Christian Anderson.

It didn't happen right away. I knew I liked the movie at first, but it wasn't love at first sight by any means. But after that initial viewing, the movie continued to stay with me, and my love and admiration for it continued to grow. I was working a convention sometime in the spring of 2014, where I had a table set up selling my Velcro the Ninja Kat books. And once someone walked past who was dressed as the Snow Queen in her blue dress from the movie, I could feel my heart skip a beat at the sight of her. I told this story to another friend of mine later that summer, and it was during our conversation that I think I realized that *Frozen* had become my favorite movie of all time.

I was just able to relate so much with the movie's story and themes and characters. And the Snow Queen in particular is among the most personally relatable characters I've ever seen in a work of fiction. I was able to feel a real connection with this movie as such, and after realizing just how much this film truly meant to me, the ideas starting coming to mind to get a tattoo to reflect that connection.

I knew I wanted something Snow Queen related, but it wasn't until I stumbled upon a particular piece of fan art that I was certain precisely what to get. The art depicted the Snow Queen during the *Let It Go* sequence in the film, just at the moment when she lets down her hair, just before she transformed her dress to blue. It's just such a striking and beautiful shot, and one that I felt captured the moment's most emotional high note, the point where the Snow Queen felt most free and able to be herself for the first time in forever.

But even after I had decided upon the design and location (I ultimately decided upon getting the image tattooed on my right ankle), I still put off getting it for a number of years. In addition to my day job, I was also donating plasma for extra income at the time, and they didn't let you donate for at least a year if you got a new tattoo. So I held off for that reason, until I was ready to make a big move in my life.

It was August of 2016, and we were mere weeks away from my 30th birthday. In addition, I was also in the process of moving down to Tampa, where I already had a job and housing lined up. So, before the big move away, and just before I turned 30, I decided to finally pull the trigger and get my *Frozen* tattoo.

Like my Sonic tattoo, this one has been one of my more popular pieces. Not too many people have seen it, but most who have have really loved it. And even after I finished getting it in the shop, there were other workers there who wanted to get a picture of it to show to people they knew would appreciate it, which is currently the only time I've had that happen for any of my tattoos. But for me personally, I was in love with the end result, and to this day it remains my favorite tattoo that I have so far.

2020
The Babymetal Tattoo

Like with Naruto, it wasn't long before I was so deep into Babymetal that I was already toying with tattoo ideas, and when I saw the promotional material for the band's 2015 world tour, which featured the band members in these really slick black metallic fox helmets and capes, I knew this was in the realm of what I wanted to get emblazoned on my skin.

It would turn out that, shortly before I had gotten into the band during the summer of 2018, they were in fact wearing outfits with this style on stage during their performances of the song *In The Name Of*. And I eventually stumbled upon an image in particular from one of these performances that just instantly spoke to me, a shot that showed the band's lead singer, Suzuka, in helmeted warrior attire holding her staff in her right hand, with her left hand placed over her chest, as she just slightly looks off to the side, and I knew this was the one.

Like the *Frozen* tattoo, I did take my time actually getting around to having this work done. It was in the summer of 2020, shortly after the covid lockdowns took effect. Euphoria had just moved to a new location, and they were staying open despite the lockdown orders, with Alain working as the sole artist in the shop at the time. I was living in Tallahassee again, and I figured this would be the perfect time to go back up to the shop and help keep their doors open by giving them my business. Plus, the masked look of the tattoo would act as a timestamp of sorts for the period in which I was getting the tattoo, and the costumes being from their 2018 tour also represented the band's style during the period in which I had initially discovered them. So it served multiple purposes of meaning and relevancy.

The design was also dark enough and large enough to where I figured it could work as a possible cover-up piece to go over my Abraham Lincoln tattoo. When I brought the idea up to my artist, he said it could be done, we'd just have to probably add some effects in the background to really cover everything up, so we decided upon a dark nighttime setting with lightning striking sporadically in the background.

I also thought the idea of this tattoo replacing the previous wrestling-based tattoo was fitting, since in many regards, my obsession with wrestling, which had been waning for some time then, had recently been replaced by my obsession with Babymetal. Even the band's producer has mentioned before that there are a number of similarities between Babymetal's presentation and professional wrestling, which I had noticed myself as well. Similarities such as all of the various characters that rotate in and out, the on-stage theatrics and physicality of their show, their ongoing storylines, and even how their bigger arena shows very much have a wrestling pay-per-view style of build and feel to them, while their smaller shows feel more reminiscent to wrestling house shows.

The cover-up took two sessions to complete, and in terms of pain, this was by far the worst yet. My leg was in so much pain afterward, I was limping for a week. I was working at a grocery store at the time, and while I usually had to move around quite a bit stocking shelves at my job, the pain was so intense that I actually had to request to take on a different task that would see me standing in place cutting fruit most of the day instead, which they thankfully obliged.

But I was pleased with the end result of the tattoo, and of course much happier than I was with the Abraham Lincoln tattoo. Though my only regret that would nag at me was the fact that, in order to completely cover up the previous tattoo, we had to make both the image itself and the background fairly dark, meaning that the tattoo still didn't really pop.

2024
Tattoo Removal

While I was significantly happier with my Babymetal tattoo, it did bother me that, for the most part, it still looked like a big black spot on my leg, as the main image didn't really pop off of the background. I spent several years toying with ideas and doing research, seeing if there was any way to address this issue with perhaps more tattoo work. In the end, though, I realized that the best option was going to be tattoo laser removal.

I was a bit hesitant about doing laser removal. I had heard that it was much more expensive than getting tattooed was, as well as much more painful. I also wasn't sure if they would be willing to do custom work, where they just remove the background of the tattoo but leave the main image intact. Thankfully, in the spring of

2024, I found a treatment center where they were willing to do precisely that, and they offered me a fairly good deal to get the work done.

So I booked my appointment, and I went up to the location. I was asked to sit down on a table, and the doc started the work. And let me tell you, what they say about the pain is absolutely true. It was instant, and it was excruciating. Halfway into the work, I had to take a break. I was exhausted from the pain, I was nauseous and feeling light headed, and I asked the doctor if this was normal. He said that it was, that my body was undergoing a lot of stress right now, and so he told me to go ahead and lay down on the table. And so I did, but my world continued to grow hazy. As he turned the laser back on and went back to work, everything turned to black...

* * *

Sometime later I woke back up on the table, but the room was dark, and I was alone. I sat up and looked down at my leg, and I was surprised to see that my entire Babymetal tattoo was gone. I was understandably upset, as this wasn't what we had agreed upon at all. So I stood up off the table and leaned down to pull my pants back up, but when I did so, I couldn't help but notice my left leg looked strangely bare as well. Further inspection would show that my Sonic tattoo was also missing, as was my *Frozen* tattoo, my Velcro tattoo, my Great Mosquito tattoo, and my Madness tattoo. I was relieved to see that the Naruto tattoo on my left shoulder remained intact, as did the old English W on my right arm.

In addition to my tattoos gone missing, my clothes had bizarrely changed, too. As I looked myself over, I soon recognized what I was wearing, as it resembled the same uniform as worn by members of the Anbu forces from Naruto, including a gray flak jacket and arm guards.

My anger was replaced by confusion, and I stepped out of the office to look for the doctor and ask him what was going on. But as I stepped through the door I was no longer in the doctor's office, but rather in a dark, strange forest of some sort. Despite no evident light, I was still able to see clearly in front of me, where a forest of trees stood illuminated in the dark before my eyes. I turned around, but the room I had just stepped through was no longer there.

At this point I figured that I must have passed out on the table, and surely I was simply dreaming all of this right now. But even so, I wanted to see how it would all play out.

Then I heard someone singing. The voice had a strength to it, and yet even so, it was as if this is what it would sound like if flowers could sing. I followed towards the sound of the voice, and as I got closer, and I heard the Japanese lyrics, I realized that I knew this song. I entered a clearing in the forest, and that's when I discovered the source of the singing. It was Suzuka, or at least someone who strongly resembled her, dressed in her warrior-like attire with her head to the sky, singing her song up to the moon above. But how could this be?

We were startled to see each other. I was suddenly starstruck, and I had to restrain myself from babbling like an idiot about how much her music meant to me. I was able to regain my composure however, and I asked her why she was here, and where exactly *here* was.

She started rambling at the mouth in Japanese, and I wasn't able to make out a word she was saying. She must have noticed my confusion, though, because eventually she stopped talking, then simply smiled and shrugged, and responded with a chuckle in English, "I don't know."

Just then, a cold breeze suddenly brushed past us, and I noticed the temperature took a rapid dip. I then looked down to my right ankle, and a realization struck me. I frantically looked around, trying to see past the trees, when suddenly I saw her. I could feel my heart skip a beat at the sight of her. There she was, the Snow Queen.

I called out to her, and she turned towards the sound of my voice. She cautiously approached, asking who we were, and where we were. But I couldn't respond. It was like my body had frozen up, and my mind went blank at the sight of her. Suzuka appeared to notice this, and so she spoke up first, once again rambling her motor mouth in Japanese. The Snow Queen looked confused, and when I was finally able to speak I explain what Suzuka was trying to say, that we were just as lost and confused as she was.

I tried to say more, but before I could get any more words out I was distracted by movement from the corner of my eye. I glanced over, and I saw a cat casually walking past. Except, it wasn't just any cat. It was *my* cat.

"*Velcro?*"

She glanced over at the sound of her name, then after a double take, she enthusiastically meowed back at me. She rushed over to my side, and I dropped down and scooped her up in my arms, hugging her tight. I could hear her purr, and

I could feel tears starting to well up in my eyes. The Snow Queen asked if I knew this cat, to which I responded of course. This was *my* cat, Velcro, who I hadn't seen in a very long time.

Suddenly we heard a rustling in the bushes nearby. We all turned toward the sound, and we were all in awe as a blue hedgehog and all his animal friends stepped out, including a fox, an echidna, a chipmunk, and a rabbit. Once they noticed us, they were quickly on their guard, but the Snow Queen was able to assure them that we were friendly. And as everyone was gathered and conversing, I took a moment to really take in the scene before me. All of the characters from the tattoos that had disappeared off my body had somehow come to life before my eyes. It was like a scene from a Saturday morning cartoon special.

The blue hedgehog's patience had appeared to reach its limit, though, as he started tapping his foot, then he spoke up, asking aloud the same question that was on everybody's mind. "Would anyone like to tell me what's going on here exactly?"

Before anyone could answer his question though, there was an *explosion*. The forest burst into flames. We all huddled together on our guard, when suddenly, we heard a sinister laughter through the fire.

We all stood our ground as we stared in the direction of the fire and laughter, when in flew a mad scientist, riding aboard his egg-shaped hover-craft vehicle. He mocked our peaceful gathering, and warned us that the time for peace was over. The blue hedgehog demanded to know what he had planned, but the mad scientist insisted that rather than tell us, he wanted to *show* us.

The hedgehog was then attacked from behind, as a large mosquito who was about the size of my fist had swooped in and landed on the back of his neck, quickly biting down on him. The hedgehog yelped at the bite, then before any us could react to what had just happened, the mosquito zipped next over to Suzuka, biting down on her neck as well. Suzuka similarly yelled out in pain, then the mosquito flew up to the mad scientist's side and landed on his shoulder.

The Snow Queen asked what just happened, when suddenly the blue hedgehog and Suzuka both fell down to their hands and knees, where they were grasping at their heads and screaming in anguish. The chipmunk asked what was going on, and demanded to know who this was who was working alongside the mad scientist.

I responded, "That's The Great Mosquito."

The Great Mosquito confirmed as I said, before informing us that in addition to biting his victims, he had infected them with a dose of Madness. He further explained that not unlike his Black Magic, the Madness would unleash the inner darkness that resided within our friends, and drive them crazy in the process. This in turn would leave them susceptible for the second phase of our enemies' plot.

"Allow me to demonstrate," the mad scientist spoke with a vile chuckle. He then shot a beam from his hovercraft down to the hedgehog, followed by a second beam which attacked Suzuka. Upon being struck by the beam, the two underwent a transformation, as they were roboticized before our eyes.

In their newly robotic forms, they stood back up to their feet, then they turned to face us, as we looked on in horror. The blue hedgehog glared at us with his menacing robotic eyes. And Suzuka now wielded her staff in hand and her spikey fox helmet over her head, as she similarly stared us down threateningly.

"We call this operation Mecha Madness," the mad scientist announced. He reveled that with our friends now fully under their control, it'd be much easier for them to capture and enslave the rest of us, too.

"We should go," said the chipmunk.

"Right," I agreed.

I scooped Velcro back into my arms, then as we all turned and ran, the Snow Queen stayed behind to use her ice powers to put out the remaining flames. She then conjured a wall of ice in an attempt to hold back our adversaries and stall them from following us. She caught back up with the rest of us, and we all ran deep into the woods, distancing ourselves as much as we could, until we heard the ice wall shatter.

We veered off to the side, and we found a place to hide and catch our breath. The fox asked what we were going to do, but he was quickly shushed, as we listened in to make sure we were no longer being pursued.

Once it appeared that the coast was clear, we huddled together to form a plan. The echidna suggested that we split up. He said that he'd take on the hedgehog, and asked the fox to hand him over a power ring.

"You're not suggesting what I think you are, are you?" the chipmunk asked him.

Before her concerns could be elaborated on though, the rabbit volunteered to go along with the echidna in order to keep him out of trouble, and we continued forward with the plan of action. The chipmunk and the fox decided that they'd take on Suzuka, then it was decided that the Snow Queen, Velcro, and I would go after the mad scientist and The Great Mosquito. It was assessed that the Snow Queen's ice powers could cancel out the mad scientist's fiery attacks, and also that I might know of a way to defeat The Great Mosquito, since I appeared to be more familiar with him.

Of course I was familiar with The Great Mosquito. I created him, after all.

* * *

With everyone aware of their tasks, we split off. The Snow Queen, Velcro, and I made our way through the forest looking for the mad scientist and The Great Mosquito. However, as we made it to a clearing where the fire had burned down the woods, we were stopped in our tracks. Standing before us was a new mysterious foe whose back was turned to us, and who was wearing a black suit and a top hat. We were on guard as the man in the top hat turned around to face us, and we were stunned by the sight of Abraham Lincoln standing there, his wrestling championship belt wrapped around his waist.

Abraham Lincoln fully turned to face us. We saw that he was shirtless under his suit jacket, which he slipped off and tossed to the side. He then unwrapped the championship belt from around his waist, and he hoisted it into the air above his head, challenging us.

I was reluctant, but I accepted his challenge, and told Velcro and the Snow Queen that I'd deal with this. As I stepped up to approach, Lincoln lowered his belt to the ground, then he reached up to pull off his top hat. He then flung the hat in my direction, but I ducked just in time to avoid the projectile strike. It went sailing behind the other two as well, but once it flew past the Snow Queen, The Great Mosquito flew out from under the hat, landing on her neck and biting down on her.

The Snow Queen screamed out in pain. Velcro swatted at The Great Mosquito, but he was quick to evade and fly away to safety. Like our other friends before, the Snow Queen dropped down to her knees, grabbing her head in agony. The more she agonized, the more her powers started to spiral out of control. Soon, a blizzard was forming in the vicinity.

I tried to aid the Snow Queen, but in my distraction, Lincoln caught me off guard, knocking me face first to the ground with a forearm to the back of my head. He rolled me over and pulled me back to my feet, and for a moment, I caught a glimpse into his eyes, where I could see the same menacing look that had been etched onto the hedgehog's and Suzuka's faces.

He had been infected by the Madness, too, I surmised.

He hit me with a knee to the gut, then he delivered a suplex, slamming me hard onto my back. I could see my own breath from the dropping temperature as I gasped from the impact.

He popped back up to his feet, then he climbed up onto a tall tree stump, where he was setting up for a high flying maneuver. He leapt off the tree stump and attempted an elbow drop, but Velcro had bitten onto my ankle and pulled me out of the way just in time to see the wrestling champion crashing onto the ground instead.

I rolled back to my feet and patted Velcro on her head. Then as Lincoln started recovering, I reared back against a tree branch, bouncing off of it and rushing towards my opponent with an attempt at a clothesline.

Lincoln ducked under to avoid my attack however, and when I turned back to face him, he kicked me in the stomach and went for a jumping cutter. I managed to counter as well though, wrapping my arms around his neck and locking him into a sleeper hold. As I strengthened my grip, slowly lowering him to the ground, I pleaded with Lincoln to fight off the Madness, telling him that I believe in him to fight back.

At that moment, I could feel a burning sensation on my right bicep, where my W tattoo was located. And in the next moment, Lincoln responded to my pleas in fluster and confusion. He asked me where he was, what was going on, and demanded to be released this instant. I did as requested, and relinquished Lincoln from my sleeper hold. He grabbed at his throat, coughing as he pulled himself back to his feet, shivering from the still brewing blizzard, and he asked me what was the meaning of this.

I explained that he had been forced into a heel turn, but thankfully appeared to have come back to his senses, though I was admittedly unsure how. I elaborated upon the mad scientist's and The Great Mosquito's plot in all of this, and asked if he would join us in taking them down and saving our friends. He responded in the affirmative, saying that that's why he was elected after all.

Then the sound of a gunshot fired.

Lincoln was stunned, and I watched in horror as the former president began to disintegrate and disappear into a haze.

"*What just happened?!*" I asked aghast.

That's when we saw him, standing just ahead with his gun pointed towards us, the man who shot Abraham Lincoln from behind: John Wilkes Booth.

I was in a state of shock at the scene that had just transpired. I asked John Wilkes Booth, "*What have you done?*"

"Nothing I haven't done before," he replied, "and that I'm not afraid to do again."

I could only shake my head at his response, as my shock soon turned to anger. I demanded to know why he was doing this. He responded that it was because I had tried to erase him, so now he was going to erase me.

He revealed his revenge scheme, saying that he was the real reason that we were all there. He said that it was bad enough that he had been covered up, but to be fully erased through laser removal was taking things too far. He said that he refused to be erased, but that if he was going to go out, then he was at least going to take everyone else out with him.

He then took aim at me with his gun.

Putting my ninja abilities to use, I gathered my chakra, and I dropped down and summoned a mud wall to rise before me, just as Booth pulled the trigger. My wall rose fast enough to block the blast, but the gun's laser caused it to disintegrate much like President Lincoln just had.

With my wall no longer there to guard me, Booth took aim once more. This time however, before he could pull the trigger, he was tripped up by Velcro, who started aggressively brushing against his legs. In his distraction, I pulled out a kunai from my back pouch, and I rushed forward to attack Booth with my blade.

Booth kicked Velcro away though, regaining his composure and firing another laser blast right at me. It was a direct hit, and I was stunned in place. However, rather than disintegrate, my body popped away in a puff of smoke, and it was replaced by a log.

What happened was that I had cast a substitution jutsu in which, unbeknownst to my enemy, I had swapped places with an object around me, in this case a log. Meanwhile, my real body was already behind Booth, who was still trying to figure it all out, when I collected my chakra and formed the lightning blade in my hand. Booth was able to hear the chirping sounds of the lightning blade, but it was too late for him to react, as I stabbed him with my jutsu from behind, thrusting my arm straight through his heart.

The gun dropped from Booth's hand, and he soon followed it as he fell to his knees and I retracted my arm from his chest. He grit his teeth as black blood that resembled ink spilled out of him, and he stubbornly insisted that I couldn't get rid of him. He turned to yell at me as I knelt down to pick up the gun, but I cut his rant off short as I took aim with the weapon.

"I'm sorry, but you were a mistake," I told him. I pulled the trigger, and as the laser hit its mark, I watched John Wilkes Booth disintegrate into the cold winds.

Velcro rushed up and rubbed against my legs, and I dropped the gun and scooped her up into my arms. I observed the intensifying blizzard, and as I scanned the area, I was able to see the other battles transpiring off in the distance. I could see the mecha hedgehog battling it out in the air against the echidna, who had since been roboticized as well, and I could see that the rabbit was laid out on the ground where their battle took place. And elsewhere, I could see Suzuka standing atop a hill, firing down rays of light from her staff, as the fox and the chipmunk continued to dodge her attacks and look for an opening. I then glanced over to the Snow Queen still on the ground, her icy winds whirling.

I looked down to Velcro in my arms, and I asked her, "What do we do?"

Velcro latched her claws around my right arm, then she playfully bit down on the W tattoo on my bicep. She then looked me straight in the eyes, and she started licking the tattoo, when the burning sensation from before had once more returned to that spot. I recalled the moment with Abraham Lincoln locked in my sleeper hold, and suddenly, an idea sprang to mind.

I let Velcro down, then I rushed over to the Snow Queen, but the closer I got, the harsher the cold winds blew. "No, stay back," she warned me, trying to protect me from her out of control powers.

But I encouraged the Snow Queen, just as I had with Lincoln. Inching my way closer, pushing against the wind, I told her that she could control her powers, and that she was strong enough to overcome the Madness that had infected her.

She looked at me horrified, unable to believe what I was saying. "I don't want to hurt you."

"You won't," I said. Then in a desperate leap I threw myself forward, and wrapped my arms around her, hugging her tight. I told her that I believed in her, and simultaneously I felt the burning again on my W tattoo.

The burning soon fizzled though, as my body started covering in ice. As I watched the light return to her eyes, she looked into mine with concern, and she wrapped her arms around me, hugging my freezing body in return. The raging storm instantly died, and I could feel my body begin to thaw.

The Snow Queen stepped back and marveled at the sight. I smiled brightly, telling her that I knew she could do it. I grabbed her hand, and I told her now we had to go and save the rest of our friends.

* * *

The three of us rushed over to the other battles. I made my way over to the chipmunk and the fox, while the Snow Queen continued ahead with Velcro, making their way to the mad scientist, who was witnessing all of the mayhem from a safe distance in his hovercraft. Meanwhile, I pulled the chipmunk aside to tell her our plan while the fox continued to keep Suzuka preoccupied.

I explained my theory of defeating the Madness infection, which would bring our friends back to their normal state of mind. I pointed to my

W tattoo, and told her the meaning of it. That it's a representation of family, and that through love, connection, and positive affirmation, we could bring our friends back from the darkness within them.

The chipmunk then nodded her head, and she told the fox to handle things over here, while she'll take care of the hedgehog. "I know what I have to do," she said, and she took off.

The fox stared up at Suzuka on the hill. As the chipmunk joined the fight against the mecha hedgehog, she opened her arms and called out to him. The fox flew towards Suzuka, and the hedgehog charged forward to attack the chipmunk. The fox then wrapped his arms around Suzuka and gave her his message, and the chipmunk similarly wrapped her arms around the hedgehog in a loving embrace, whispering something into his ear as well. I observed as Suzuka and the blue hedgehog both appeared to come back to their senses, and with all well on this end, I hurried over to help out the Snow Queen and Velcro.

By the time I made it there, the Snow Queen had already succeeded in freezing the mad scientist and his machinery. I hopped into the vehicle and shoved the frozen foe out of the way, then I took the controls and fired the beam at our friends, reversing their roboticization and returning them back to their normal state.

"Watch out!" I then heard the rabbit yell out.

I turned around just in time to see The Great Mosquito zipping straight for me. However, before he could reach me, Velcro leaped up and swatted the bug down and proudly pinned him to the ground.

All of our friends then gathered around, and as we looked down at the defeated mad scientist and Great Mosquito, the Snow Queen asked aloud the same question that was on everybody's mind, "Now   what?"

Velcro rubbed up against my legs again, and I picked her up once more. She purred in my arms, then she pressed her head against my chest, just over my heart. I nodded, and I uttered, "Of course."

I explained my revelation to the group, telling them how they had all come from my tattoos, and so the only way out of this place is for all of us to come back together again as one. "But it has to be *all* of us," I insisted, referring to the two villains on the ground.

There was an understandable pushback to my suggestion, as the others couldn't tolerate coming together with our enemies who had just pitted us against each other. However, I told them that the darkness was a part of us, and the only way for us to leave this place and move on is by uniting as one.

Reluctantly, everyone agreed, and we let up the mad scientist and The Great Mosquito, who awkwardly joined us as we all stood in a circle holding hands. Suzuka began singing a song about coming together as one, and at her insistence, we all sang along.

I then felt a burning sensation on my ribs, and I pulled up my shirt to see that my Madness tattoo had returned to its place. Next I felt that sensation on my shoulder, and my ninja uniform that I had been wearing disappeared, and I was back in my normal clothes.

I felt the burning on my wrist, then The Great Mosquito disappeared and reappeared on my wrist like magic. Then I felt the heat on my leg, and one by one, I watched as the blue hedgehog, the fox, the echidna, the chipmunk, the rabbit, and the mad scientist all faded away from sight and back onto my leg.

I then had a moment of panic, as I realized what was coming next. I picked Velcro up into my arms and I held her tight, and I told her goodbye, just as I had so many years ago. She purred reassuringly, and as she pressed up against my chest, I watched as she slipped out of my arms and into the warm burning feeling over my heart.

I then looked over to the Snow Queen and Suzuka. I stepped up to the Snow Queen, and I told her how happy I was to have had this time with her. I told her how I wish it could be longer, but that it was time for me to let her go. She clasped my hands, and as I pulled her close to me I looked deeply into her eyes. Then as I wrapped my arms around her one last time, I was left hugging myself, as she too had disappeared, returning onto my ankle as the burn dissipated.

I was suddenly overwhelmed with sadness, which Suzuka could clearly see. She stepped over and lifted my chin, and she reassured me that no matter what difficulties lie ahead, that we'll always get through it together. I smiled at her words, and she smiled back. She said, "See you!" And I watched as she left like the rest, resuming her place just over my right knee.

I closed my eyes then...

* * *

When I reopened them, I was once more back on the table in the doctor's office. After the doctor had finished with the tattoo removal procedure, I inspected my body, and all of the tattoos appeared to be back where they belonged.

It was all a dream after all. And yet, it all felt so real.

A MEMORY
OF SNOW

In the winter of 2018, I flew up from Florida to New York and visited my family who lived up there. My brother, Tim, let me stay at his place, and it was a pleasant visit for the most part.

On the day that I arrived, it had unexpectedly snowed. The roads hadn't been prepared for the snow yet, and so there were cars drifting all over the place. We even had to get outside and help a few people get their cars unstuck from the snow. On the one hand, it was somewhat of a disastrous situation. But on the other, this was actually the first time I had seen snow in person since I was a little boy myself.

Growing up in Tallahassee, Florida, it very rarely snowed. But one time, when I was very young, we actually did get snow. In fact, perhaps one of my earliest memories that I still retain was of this magical time in the snow. I remember playing with my brothers outside, and tossing snowballs at one another. And I remember the uncomfortable feeling of snow getting caught inside my jacket. So to see snow again for the first time since I was a kid brought those memories of old rushing back to me, and it put a wondrous smile on my face.

Tim and his wife Kristen were very warm and welcoming. However, my nephew, Cam, didn't appear nearly so thrilled with my being there. He had a tendency to be rude, and he didn't even call me Uncle, referring to me by first name only. In a way, I suppose I perhaps deserved that, seeing how estranged I had become with my family for so long, but that didn't change the fact that it still hurt. Still though, I tried not to let it get to me too badly, and brushed it off as kids just being kids.

Just as I had my passions as a kid, Cam also had his. And his big thing was video games, which I could certainly relate to. While I don't play video games anymore, I was very much a gamer back when I was Cam's age. He tended to gravitate more towards games that allowed for a lot of customization, such as games like Little Big Planet.

And as it would also turn out, like me, he was also quite a big fan of Sonic the Hedgehog.

While I've carried on in my fanaticism of certain properties as an adult, when I was a kid I definitely had different things I was passionate about. At various times in my childhood, I was practically obsessed with Teenage Mutant Ninja Turtles, Mighty Morphin Power Rangers, and Pokémon, among other things. But of all the things I was a passionate fan of as a kid, the one that continued to stay with me even well into adulthood was Sonic the Hedgehog.

Upon finding out about this shared passion that we had in common, Cam invited me to play Sonic the Hedgehog 4 with him, and I of course obliged. He played as the titular character, while I played as his fox sidekick, and we had a great time making our way through the game together. It reminded me of when I was a kid playing two player on Sonic the Hedgehog 2 with my brothers, or other various multiplayer games we might've indulged in back then. And getting to re-experience this with my nephew felt like a true bonding moment.

* * *

The following day, I joined Kristen and Cam as they walked to the grocery store to pick up some things. Afterwards, when we returned back to the house, we realized that I had accidentally locked us all outside. Tim was at work, so it would be some time before he got back home to let us all in. And so, since we couldn't go indoors, we turned to all of the fresh snow in the yard, and Kristen suggested that Cam and I should build a snowman.

And so we did.

We rolled up a large ball of snow for the lower body and packed it tight. Then we rolled up the next stack for the upper body and struggled to lift it on top. By the time we got to the snowman's head, the landlord thankfully showd up and was able to unlock the door for us. Kristen went inside and grabbed some items to give our snowman the finishing touches, including a top hat, a scarf, a carrot, a pipe, and some buttons, then Cam and I posed with our snowman as she took a picture of us after all our hard work.

We were proud of our snowman, and I couldn't help but wonder if perhaps this would be a memory that would stay with Cam, much like my own memory of snow had stayed with me after all these years. But for now, since the door was unlocked again, we went in out of the cold and hopped back onto some more video games. By the time Tim made it back home from work, we were knee deep in another game of Sonic the Hedgehog, making new memories to someday look back on.

I would like to thank everyone who directly contributed to the creation of this book, including Christine Celenski, M.H. Smith, Adam Widdop, and my Uncle Bob and Aunt Laurie.

And I would especially like to thank my mom, without whom this book would not have been possible.

Growing up, Chris Widdop would constantly escape into the fantasy world that was his vivid imagination, where he took part in many adventures. And now, Chris wants nothing more than to share those adventures with the world.